CONTENTS

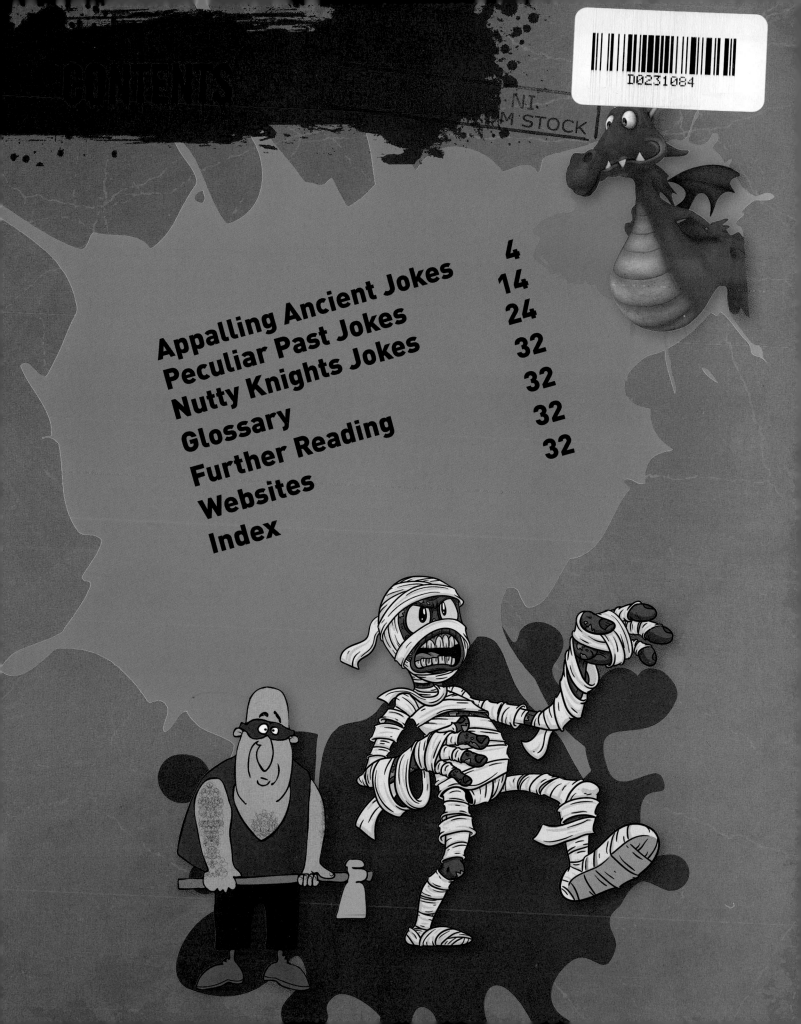

APPALLING ANCIENT JOKES

What does a caveman's wife give his wife on valentine's day? Lots of hugs and kisses.

What do you call a caveman who's been buried since the Stone Age?
Peat.

What are Ancient Egyptian parents called?
Mummies and deadies.

Why did the T. rex eat a caveman?
He was really hungry, man!

4

Why did the Roman colosseum have to close?
The lions had eaten up all the prophets!

What do you get in a five-star pyramid?
A tomb with a view.

Which Roman emperor is the windiest?
Au-gust-us.

What do you call armoured pyjamas?
Knight nighties.

What do you get if you cross a pharaoh with a mechanic?
A toot and car man.

Did you hear about the angry mummy?
He flipped his lid.

A Roman emperor asked his soothsayer to tell him the future. "I'm afraid your wife is going to die very suddenly," said the soothsayer. Two days later, the emperor's wife died. The emperor was very angry and ordered the soothsayer to come to him immediately. "Let's see if you can guess when you are going to die," said the emperor. Terrified, the soothsayer replied: "I don't know when I am going to die... but I do know that you will die two days later." The emperor left him alone!

8

What do you call a sleeping T-rex?
A dino-snore.

What game did the Ancient Greeks play?
Hydra and seek.

What do you call a Roman emperor with a cold?
Julius Sneezer.

Why were Ancient Egyptian children confused?
Because their daddies were mummies.

What do you call a friendly pharaoh?
A chummy mummy.

How fast can a caveman run? It depends on the size of the dinosaur chasing him!

Why does it say "1286 BC" on the Ancient Egyptian's tomb? It's the registration number of the chariot that ran him over!

Why do mummies make excellent spies? They're good at keeping things under wraps.

Why did the mummy leave his tomb after 3,000 years?

Because he thought he was old enough to leave home.

Why didn't the Ancient Egyptian care when his boat sank?

He was in de Nile.

Why did Blackbeard wear headphones?
He liked listening to pirate radio.

What did the pirate say when his wooden leg got stuck in the freezer?
"Shiver me timbers!"

How did Columbus's men sleep on their ships?
With their eyes shut.

Why did the cowboy die with his boots on?
Because he didn't want to stub his toes when he kicked the bucket.

Why was George Washington buried at Mount Vernon?
Because he was dead.

What do you get when you cross a president of the United States with a shark?
Jaws Washington.

Why did Christopher Columbus sail to America?
Because it was too far to swim!

Who conquered half the world, laying eggs along the way?
Attila the Hen.

How much did the pirate pay for his peg leg and hook?
An arm and a leg.

What did the pirate cry as he fell overboard?
Water way to go!

An ancestor of mine went to America on the Mayflower. Really? Which rat was he?

Where was the Declaration of Independence signed? At the bottom.

A pirate with an eye patch, a hook and a peg leg walks into a tavern. The bartender says, "You look like you've been in lots of sea battles. How did you get the peg leg?" The pirate answers, "Arr, a cannonball blew me leg right off!" "Wow!" says the bartender, "And how about the hook?" "Arr, me hand was eaten by a shark on the high seas!" "That's amazing! And the eye patch?" "Arr, a seagull pooped in me eye." Confused, the bartender asks, "How can you lose your eye from seagull poo?" "Well, it was me first day with the hook."

17

Why do dragons breathe fire?
Because they don't like raw meat.

What happens when a queen burps?
She gets a royal pardon.

How was King Henry VIII different from normal husbands?
He married his wives first, and axed them afterwards.

What did the ghost of Queen Bess say as it floated through the terrified woman's bedroom?
Don't worry, I'm just passing through.

What did the dragon say when he saw St George in his shining armour?
Oh no, not more canned food!

Why didn't Henry VIII's marriage last?
At least two of his wives found him a pain in the neck.

Lady: We had boar for dinner last night.
Knight: Wild?
Lady: Let's just say he wasn't too happy.

25

Which British queen belched the most?
Queen Hic-toria.

It was once the custom for rich people to wear a fancy collar known as a ruff. The heir to the throne wore a small but fancy ruff, known as a dandy ruff. It was so tight that he fainted, and fell from the top of a tower. This proves that a little dandy ruff can cause the heir to fall out!

Which knight loved to throw unexpected parties?
Sir Prise!

What does an executioner read in the morning?
The noose-paper.

Why did the knight run around screaming for a can opener?
He had a bee in his suit of armour.

Why didn't Anne Boleyn stand still when she was being executed?
She wanted to run around the block.

The duke and the count had a fight.
The duke was out for the count.

Which British queen was the fattest?
Mary, Queen of Scones.

Why did Henry VIII need an oxygen tank?
Because he couldn't breathe with no heir.

Where did Anastasia go?
I don't know. She must have been Romanov.

Why do dragons sleep all day? So they can fight knights.

In days of old
When knights were bold,
Before toilets were invented,
They left their load
Along the road
And walked away contented.

How do you get ahead in life? Become a royal executioner.

What do you call a tiny man in a tin suit?
A mite in shining armour.

Why did the knight always carry a bookmark?
He didn't want to lose his page!

Three knights came across a dragon in the forest. The dragon said, "I'm going to eat you." The first knight said, "Wait! Let's make a deal. Let each of us tell you something we think you can't do. If you can do it, you may eat us." The dragon agreed to the deal. Said the first knight: "Go to the barn and eat 16 rooms full of hay." The dragon did it. Said the second knight: "Drink half the water in the ocean." The dragon did this. The third knight burped and said: "Catch it and paint it green."

Teacher: If William Braveheart Wallace was alive today, he would be looked on as a remarkable man.
Pupil: Yes, he'd be more than 600 years old!

Why did some kings like uprisings? They found them a peasant surprise.

Why did the queen have to tell her eldest son to stop being rude? She was having a bad heir day!

31

Further Reading

Connolly, Sean. *Laugh Out Loud! The School's Cool Joke Book*. Franklin Watts, 2012.

Deary, Terry. *Horribly Hilarious Joke Book*. Scholastic, 2013.

Weitzman, Ilana, and others. *Jokelopedia*. Workman Publishing Company, revised edition 2013.

Websites

www.ducksters.com/jokesforkids/
A safe site with jokes on many categories, from history to sport, nature to some very silly jokes!

www.kidsjokes.co.uk/jokes/other/history.html
Some jokes that have been dug up since the dawn of time.

Index